Career Quest

EXPLORING GAMING INDUSTRY CAREERS

SHERRY HOWARD AND MARI BOLTE

TWENTY-FIRST CENTURY BOOKS / MINNEAPOLIS

Twenty-First Century Books™
An imprint of Lerner Publishing Group, Inc.
241 First Avenue North
Minneapolis, MN 55401 USA

For reading levels and more information, look up this title at www.lernerbooks.com.

Main body text set in Bembo Std Regular.
Typeface provided by Monotype Typography.

Library of Congress Cataloging-in-Publication Data

Names: Howard, Sherry author | Bolte, Mari, author.
Title: Exploring gaming industry careers / Sherry Howard and Mari Bolte.
Description: Minneapolis : Twenty-First Century Books, 2026. | Series: Career quest | Includes bibliographical references and index. | Audience term: juvenile | Audience: Ages 11–18 | Audience: Grades 7–9 | Summary: "How does someone become a pro gamer or the person behind the game? The gaming industry includes programmers, engineers, writers, artists, animators, players, and more. Learn more about this exciting field"—Provided by publisher.
Identifiers: LCCN 2024037252 (print) | LCCN 2024037253 (ebook) | ISBN 9798765644195 library binding | ISBN 9798765684894 paperback | ISBN 9798765682814 epub
Subjects: LCSH: Video games industry—Juvenile literature | Video games—Design—Vocational guidance—Juvenile literature
Classification: LCC HD9993.E452 H68 2026 (print) | LCC HD9993.E452 (ebook) | DDC 338.4/77948—dc23/eng/20241205

LC record available at https://lccn.loc.gov/2024037252
LC ebook record available at https://lccn.loc.gov/2024037253

Manufactured in the United States of America
2-1014438-52445-5/4/2026

CONTENTS

INTRODUCTION

The average gamer plays around an hour each day. That's a lot of time jumping, crouching, shooting, dodging, puzzle-solving, and more. There are many ways to turn that love of video games into a career. Someone in the gaming industry created every aspect of your gaming experience, from the buttons on the controller to the characters you control to the music that plays. If you're a skilled player with the drive to compete, you could even turn playing games into a career.

The gaming industry is more than simple entertainment. It's a dynamic, billion-dollar business that spans the globe, with a wide variety of jobs that cover a range of interests, skills, and talents. Professionals get to turn their hobbies into passions and see their work come to life. There are more than two hundred different jobs related to the video game industry.

Programmers write the computer code that brings characters and worlds to the screen. They work with producers, directors, and artists to develop compelling stories and beautiful graphics. They use coding languages and software framework tools called game engines to build projects from the ground up.

Artists create the 2D and 3D art in games, working with instructions from writers and designers. They create every part of the game players see, including wall and floor textures, the fabric and metal that make up a character's armor, and even grass blowing in the wind. Video games will always need artists. Without them, games would literally look like nothing. The US Bureau of Labor Statistics projects that jobs for special effects artists and illustrators will grow 4 percent between 2023 and 2033.

In 2024, 21 percent of adults between the ages of eighteen and twenty-nine spent six to ten hours per week gaming.

If people don't know about something, they won't know to buy it. Marketers promote games, telling people why the game is unique and why they will want to play it. They create campaigns to excite people about the game. In 2024 the video game market was valued at $200 billion, with projected growth of up to $600 billion by 2030. But people only have so much extra money. Choosing which games to hype and deciding the target market for a game can be a high-pressure job, but some people thrive in this fast-paced environment.

Games must be fun to play and free from bugs, glitches, or other problems that might encourage players to turn them off. Testers spend hours playing games and looking for problems. They record any issues they have and leave suggestions about how to fix them. They may play through certain sections or scenarios repeatedly to trigger known issues. Sometimes the job might seem dull—but it's important, guaranteeing frustration-free play for everyone.

Streaming has changed the way people consume video games. Before gamers got together with friends at arcades or at home to play their favorite titles. The people who talked about the industry publicly worked for gaming companies. Now anyone with a webcam, a headset, and an internet connection can go live to talk about their favorite (or least favorite) game, chat with other players anywhere in the world, and even earn a little extra money depending on how many people are watching.

Streamers and other players range from casual to pro. Some just play for fun. Others can take their playing to the next level by entering esports competitions. Smaller tournaments for cash prizes can be played at home. Top-tier

Video games have gone beyond entertainment. They are now a billion-dollar industry.

players travel to national or international competitions. Huge crowds gather to watch these multiplayer battles in real time. And the winners receive huge payouts. Johan Sundstein, also known as N0tail, earned more than $7 million by 2024, making him the richest esports player in the world.

The next generation of gaming consoles is always in the works. Hardware engineers build computer systems and see which physical components work best together. They research new tools and figure out how to integrate computer circuits so that the computer hardware and software cooperate. They make sure that new consoles can run both the simplest and most complex of games.

This book covers what it takes to enter the video game industry, reasons to consider such a career, and some of the challenges that you might face. It will also explore some of the most popular jobs out there and help you pick the one that is right for you.

CHAPTER ONE

Play for Pay

Computer scientists in the 1950s and 1960s started creating simple games with the basic computers at their disposal. The first arcade game then came out in 1971. Soon, many video games could be found in arcades, with people lining up to try their hand at being a hero for the low price of twenty-five cents. For the next decade-plus, friends met at arcades and competed to see who could come away with the highest score.

The first at-home console came out in 1972. Throughout the 1970s, games continued to enter the home. Owning a video game console became a badge of honor. Companies battled to release the newest gaming system and with it, a large catalog of games. Then the advent of handheld gaming late in the decade allowed people to bring their favorite games anywhere they went. By the 1990s, more people were spending money on gaming than ever. Companies that devoted all their time to video games popped up everywhere. Graphics went from flat, simple pixels to more realistic 3D pictures. The concepts, which were once limited to simple strategies or passing single levels at a time, were now fleshed out to become the first-person shooters, massive multiplayer online (MMO), role-playing, and survival horror games we know today. Designing, selling, and testing video games was suddenly a huge industry.

A lot has changed since then. Graphics are more complex, games are longer and more detailed, the genres have expanded, and the ways people can play together continue to grow. But one thing remains the same—how much people love playing them. Video game sales in 2023 amounted to more than $57 billion. What started as casual entertainment at home has grown to a huge, international arena. With billions of people playing games, more people than ever are working in the field to create and improve them. As Columbia University states, "No matter how we look at it, video games will be one of the biggest job creators of the future." But what are the benefits of working in the industry?

Anyone Can Enter the Arena

There are many types of jobs you can do in the video game industry. Creative people who love writing or art might be inspired to create epic tales that may branch into huge franchises, such as *Pokémon* or *The Legend of Zelda*. Anyone who likes working with their hands might find themselves involved with the future of consoles—designing machines, manufacturing computer chips, or troubleshooting new builds. And there are always people needed to sell games, to coordinate between game creators and game publishers, and to play the finished game!

High Demand

The number of jobs in the video game industry continues to rise, growing nearly 13 percent annually. About thirty-two thousand new jobs are expected to be added between 2023 and 2029. New formats, such as mobile games, help drive that growth by drawing in more casual players and enhancing the variety of available games. The total value of the video game market—which includes all aspects of gaming, from subscriptions to mobile gaming—is expected to surpass $720 billion globally by 2032.

Flexibility

Working in a tech-forward industry comes with certain benefits, such as workspace flexibility. Remote work grew in popularity during the early COVID-19 pandemic, and many gaming studios have embraced allowing employees to work from home, either part- or full-time. In 2023 Deconstructor of Fun, a site for gaming professionals, sent out a survey asking about remote work. Nearly 40 percent of their respondents were fully remote, with another 21 percent coming into the office once a week or less. Hybrid workers, who often work in the office one or more days a week but not every day, made up another third of the overall total. One anonymous responder said their current studio "handled it the best because they make room for us to navigate what works best for us and provide real support through the challenges to get a positive outcome." This kind of flexibility can lead to higher job satisfaction and a larger pool of jobs to choose from.

Fresh Eyes

In 2024 GameDev Reports noted that 56 percent of game developers have been working in the industry for ten years or less. Getting a job at Nintendo, Epic, or Ubisoft might seem daunting. But there are nearly four hundred video game companies located in California alone. Small indie games are the biggest source of new games on Steam, a digital distribution service for personal computer (PC) gaming. In 2023 alone, indie publishers put out 13,790 games. The major and mid-range companies, also known as AAA and AA respectively, released a combined 181 games that same year. With so many developers in the field, there are many job opportunities for young professionals entering the industry.

Engaging Work

Working on video games can be rewarding. For many workers, seeing people playing and enjoying something they helped make motivates them to keep creating. Many people in the gaming industry are also gamers themselves, which offers additional opportunities to feel fulfilled. Making something you would play yourself is often extra satisfying!

Learning Opportunities

Gaming industry professionals are constantly learning how to use a different software engine, a new algorithm to control non-playable characters (NPCs), and other tools. Learning these additional skills and tools can help workers advance their careers in the future.

Evolving technology is creating more jobs too. Yves Jacquier, the executive director at Ubisoft Montreal, said, "The way we made games in 2004 has changed a lot in the past 18 years. In 2004, a big game was made by tens of people collocated [grouped] in the same studio. Today, a big game requires hundreds of people often located in different studios."

A Shot at Fame

Only a chosen few find fame in Hollywood, but there are other ways ordinary people can gain a huge following. Streaming is one. Streaming sites such as Twitch connect gamers to potential fans who love watching them play. The most-followed streamer on Twitch is Richard Tyler Blevins, also known as Ninja. He has nineteen million followers and makes $500,000 a month between his Twitch and YouTube channels.

But being a face on camera isn't the only way to get your name out there. If you play a lot of games, the names Tim Cain, Stieg Hedlund, Scott Orr, Tim Sweeney, or Shigeru Miyamoto may sound familiar to you. They are computer programmers and designers who created some of the most popular video games of all time.

Frontline of the Future

Billions of people—no matter their age, location, gender, or financial background—love playing video games. They play shooting games, puzzle games, building games, strategy games, and more. They play alone and with friends, on- and offline. With such a wide range of interests spread out over decades, video games—and the people who make them possible—aren't going anywhere.

Hit "Start" on Women's Roles in Games

In 2009 women made up only 6 percent of the gaming industry. By 2020 they had taken over 22 percent of the workforce. And about 48 percent of all gamers are women. Despite these numbers, the online organization Women in Games reported that women filled only 16 percent of the executive teams in the top fifteen global gaming companies in 2023. And women working in any esports role—whether as a player or otherwise—made up less than 5 percent of the workforce.

Not only are women underrepresented in the job force—but they are also underpaid. In 2024 the marketing company DesignRush pulled and studied data from the US Census Bureau. They found that, on average, women are paid 82.5 percent of men's salaries. The pay difference amounts to around forty-one days of unpaid work every year.

Men also get more of a voice in games. A study by Cardiff University and the University of Glasgow found that 94 percent of all games give male characters more dialogue than women, even if the playable characters in the game are primarily women.

Many organizations hope to change these statistics. Women in Games was founded to build a diverse community across social media, providing an engaging space for women working in gaming and esports to make connections with other professionals. As more women join the gaming industry, games will hopefully start to have more gender diversity too.

CHAPTER TWO

Choose Your Character: The Builders

Game making is the pinnacle of teamwork, and even a small contribution adds to the quality of the whole. Imagine each gaming industry job as a character in a game. At first, you know a few details about them. But as you play, you gain experience points, and more of their story unlocks. Getting to the point in your life where you're ready for a job is like getting to the final boss. You want to be as prepared as possible!

Let's start with builders. Someone has to turn an idea into a playable game. The software needs to be created and tested, and the hardware must be advanced enough to make the graphics and other gameplay elements look and work their best. Programmers and engineers work with the goal of building a game that people enjoy from the moment they hit the "on" button to the moment they beat the final boss.

Some *computer hardware engineers* start out self-taught. Around one-third of all PC gamers built their own computer. Others combine classroom knowledge gained in college with on-the-job training. They research, design, build, and

Wanted: Dream Job

Getting a job in the video game industry can seem like a dream since just getting a foot in the door can be difficult. One of the most important factors to remember as you learn about the careers in this field is that staying current isn't optional. Just as many professionals have to learn new tools or skills, so will gaming professionals. And even if your dream is to be a streamer or a game developer for an already-famous franchise, remember that there are thousands of games published every year and many different professionals involved in making them. After all, a person created every part of the game that you read, hear, control, or experience. Staying on top of tech and trends will give you a professional boost.

test computers and gaming systems. Computer hardware engineering is a growing industry, with around 4,600 job openings every year and 7 percent industry growth expected between 2023 and 2033, which is faster than average. Their median salary is $138,000 per year, or $66.38 per hour.

Programmers and *software engineers* work with artists and designers. They use computer code to bring the artists' vision

Some jobs involve making video games. Others improve the gameplay experience. They might fix gaming hardware or even make it better.

to life and ensure the game runs properly. Someone in this department creates every prompt, command, movement, and action.

There are a variety of different programmers and software engineers. *Gameplay programmers* write the code for every interaction in the game. If your character picks up an item, they program that. If the character talks to another character, fights a monster, or goes swimming, they program that too. A background in computer science or programming, knowledge of 2D and 3D animation software, and effective problem-solving skills make a strong gameplay programmer. They make a high salary, averaging from $93,000 to $129,000.

Graphics programmers put images on the screen. They work with designers and producers to make sure the object looks like it fits in the game and that it realistically interacts with other objects—such as a pile of barrels that sits in a corner that might break or fall over. Thorough understanding of the coding language C/C++ is essential, as well as the ability to work well with others, especially since engineers and artists might have different visions for the same thing. Graphics programmers make an average of $70,000 per year, with more experienced programmers earning $90,000 or more.

Tools programmers set up the graphics and gameplay engineers with the software they need to create and build the game. They work with the rest of the team to find out what they need to make their jobs more streamlined. Tools engineers do not usually work directly with the game, but their work keeps the rest of the team on track. The average base pay for tools engineers is around $75,000, but some make $160,000 or more.

Network programmers make online gaming possible. When

you play online with others, the information on your screen—such as health information, locations, and usernames—is the same for everyone. This is possible because of the work network programmers do. Knowledge of servers and operating system software is crucial since the game's code needs to be connected and integrated across both physical and virtual servers. Network programmers make between $63,000 and $83,000 per year, although numbers can trend much higher depending on location and role.

Artificial intelligence (AI) programmers make games feel unique and believable. NPCs must behave like real people, reacting to things happening around them as though they have human emotions. They write programs that tell the NPCs how to respond to the game world. There is even new AI tech that runs on the cloud and collects and responds to players in real time. Knowledge of how people are likely to behave in given situations is an important skill AI programmers need. Reasoning and problem-solving skills are also essential. The salary for this job is around $120,000 a year.

User interface (UI) and *user experience (UX) engineers* streamline the player's experience with the game. They make sure the game seems interactive and immersive for the players as the players explore worlds, chop down trees, or fight enemies. UI engineers focus on visual parts of the game, such as menus and the head's up display (HUD). The HUD is a status bar that tells the player real-time information, such as how much health or mana they have left, which items they have equipped, or enemy locations. There is only so much the human brain can process at once, so HUDs that are too busy can detract from gameplay. UX engineers must figure out ways to break up that status information—and other

AI and the Gaming Industry

A study in 2023 showed that 99 percent of gamers agreed that AI NPCs enhance gameplay, and 81 percent would spend more money on games that had them. That same year, Xbox and Inworld, a leading AI developer, teamed up to develop technology to power AI NPCs. Inworld also has an engine to add real-time AI to gameplay.

AI can help enhance graphics in a game. It can combine real images with images in the game to make them look smoother, shinier, and more believable. AI lighting figures out how light rays bounce off objects to make shadows and reflection.

Some believe the future of AI is letting it create for us. It could be used to replace older graphics with new ones or to invent a new game mechanic. It might even be able to think up and generate new games.

One of the biggest concerns regarding AI in creative fields is intellectual property ownership. AI pulls from what already exists as source material. It uses photos, art, characters, and mechanics from the real world without crediting creators or identifying original ideas. AI also does not understand harmful stereotypes or social issues such as discrimination based on race or gender. The annual State of the Game Industry survey found that 84 percent of game developers were concerned about ethical AI.

Another concern is that AI may replace human workers. In 2023 more than ten thousand developers lost their jobs, with even more in danger the following year. In response, more workers are pushing for unionization, which would protect them from mass layoffs and being replaced by AI.

interactive bits—in a way that's easy to take in as it happens. Both positions require strong problem-solving skills. UI and UX engineers make anywhere from $74,000 to $125,000 a year, depending on experience, demands, and locations.

Online and *multiplayer engineers* are essential to the gaming world. With 77 percent of gamers going online to play with friends, it's important that games perform seamlessly across different systems, servers, and platforms. Information needs to be synchronized so no player has an advantage over another. Will someone playing *Fortnite* on a cell phone have the same experience as someone playing on an Xbox at home? Being fluent in C++ and able to debug games and systems are essential for this position. Pay averages around $90,500.

Are you interested in building game hardware or software as a career? A college degree is required for any of these jobs. Many gaming engineers have degrees in computer science or software engineering. Finding the program that fits your needs is an important first step toward any job in game development. Some colleges and universities—and even high schools—offer degrees specifically related to game development. For example, in 2021, Long Island High School for the Arts began offering game design programs to their students. Curriculum writer Nelle Stokes said, "This is one of the biggest industries in our country right now. And students just 'get it.' They are fluent in this language and have an ease of using digital." Some of the top colleges for game development degrees are the University of Southern California in Los Angeles, Carnegie Mellon University in Pittsburgh, the University of Utah in Salt Lake City, Georgia Institute of Technology in Atlanta, and the Rochester Institute of Technology in Rochester, New York.

Computer engineers must have problem-solving skills and an attention to detail. They must also be good at communicating and working with others.

People can also earn certifications through colleges or software programs, such as Unity, Apple, or Adobe. Certificates give students a more in-depth understanding of specialized areas that relate to the job. Another type of continuing education is coding bootcamps, which are online sessions that teach different coding languages, such as Python or C/C++. Most graduates of coding boot camps report a salary boost of around $25,000.

CHAPTER THREE

Climbing the Skills Tree: The Creatives

Video games don't come out of nowhere. They start out as an idea in someone's mind. Then creative writers, illustrators, animators, and designers craft stories, characters, and art to make an imaginary world real.

Writers create the game's main story. They also develop backstories for the characters, as well as any dialogue. But the writer doesn't have complete freedom. The words must align with every aspect of the game, including the mission, the feel of the art, and the overall world. Some games take place in historic settings, while others are part of an already-established world. The way characters speak or act must match that. An authentic script adds to the quality of the game, while creative storytelling makes the narrative fun to follow. Writers must have attention to detail, effective research skills, and the ability to take criticism and feedback well.

Many video game writing jobs require at least a high school degree and an advanced degree in screenwriting or creative writing. Building a portfolio, including examples of video game writing, is essential so employers can see your talent. Knowing how to code and how video games are created is helpful too. With how much collaboration writers must do, knowing what colleagues in different departments do and how to communicate with them is a huge part of the job.

Video Game Media

The movie industry seems like a glamorous, high-earning place to work. Between streaming services and Hollywood investing in the creation of high-budget, computer-generated imagery-heavy films, nothing seems bigger than movies. But the gaming industry is quickly catching up. And more people are getting into gaming every day. From partnering with celebrities such as Lady Gaga, 21 Savage, and Marshmello to entering the worlds of movie and music production—*The Super Mario Bros. Movie* is the highest-grossing video game movie of all time, with $1.3 billion in earnings at the box office—there are plenty of ways the gaming industry can grow.

Entry-level writers can expect to earn as little as $25,000 per year, with experienced writers topping out around $80,000. There are a handful of writers who are part of elite game franchises and have made millions. But this is rare, and even then, the writers are paid for their work but usually do not earn royalties or other continuing payments, even if the game is a continued success. Most writers are also freelancers, meaning they are hired to work on a specific project but not as full-time employees at a company. This can make the job market feel less stable or secure.

Most video game writers start out in non-gaming careers, and many work in a variety of fields, including scriptwriting.

But writing can be rewarding. Seeing fans care about characters you have created can be a huge ego boost. Freelancing gives many opportunities to work on a variety of projects too. No job is ever the same. Video game writing has also improved since the early 2000s, with video games featuring richer, more complex stories—largely due to the work of professional writers. As more information is collected, story quality continues to increase, and the value of this position is appreciated, salaries may change, and the job market may become more stable.

Coders and game engineers build the game settings. But *artists* are the first to bring a game's visuals to life. They sketch the first concepts and complete the final animations. They must work closely with every other department—each has its own job, but artists tie all their ideas together. Think about your favorite game. Does it have a distinctive art style? That can make it stand out among the crowd.

Meet and Greet

Networking can be a good way to meet people in the industry. Go to game developer conferences or join professional game developers associations. Some companies offer internships as an introduction to the game-making process. Interns receive mentorship from senior members, learning the process and assisting along the way. Some internships are paid, but others offer experience only. Companies often post internship listings and application requirements on their own websites or on online job boards.

An artist typically focuses on just one part of the game's art. *Concept artists* create the first sketches of the game, from the characters to the environments. Concept art helps drive interest in new and upcoming games, and the whole team uses that art throughout development. The finished look may barely resemble the concept art by the time the game is complete, but it is the most important part of the whole process. Concept artists must be good at following directions and have an art style with a clear vision. Art can feel personal, so being able to take criticism well and make requested changes is valuable.

The pay for concept artists varies. Some are paid by piece, with prices ranging as low as $100 for a simple sketch to $1,000 or more for more detailed art. Concept art used for marketing purposes might be sold for many times that, and artists who work for major companies may make into six figures.

The *2D* and *3D artists* create all the visual elements in the game using computers and the concept art. They model animation and textures of every animal, plant, building, object, and character. Expertise using editing tools and content generation software is essential. Animators take the artists' work a step further, bringing it to life with animation and motion capture technology. A 3D artist tends to make more money than a 2D artist because the computer and math skills needed are more complex. The 2D art uses lines and curves to create vectors. The 3D art uses pixels to build mosaics and add depth. A 2D artist makes around $67,851 per year, and a 3D artist's salary is closer to $84,000.

A video game is only as good as its setting. Characters need scenes and locations with which to interact, and *environmental artists* create the walls, forests, levels, and other framework for the story to build upon. If the game you play seems like one that could exist in our world, its environmental artist has done their job well.

Building a portfolio of your best work is essential if you want to pursue a career in the arts.

Lighting is important to a game's realism. It can also enhance drama, setting the mood. A brightly lit castle appears much more friendly than one illuminated by firelight. Players need to see what's going on, even during night scenes or in dense fog. If the character carries a lamp, torch, or flashlight, the light source is constantly moving. *Lighting artists* make sure lights and shadows behave naturally. Photography skills will help develop your eye for lighting. Studying the science of light to understand why certain colors appear in nature will help too. The average salary for a lighting artist ranges from $53,000 to $61,000, depending on experience, location, and employer.

Artists do not always need a formal degree to find work. A strong portfolio is the best way to show employers you can get the job done. Submit art samples with your job application that match the feel of the project. Knowledge of coding, art software such as Adobe, graphics software such as Blender, and game engines such as Unreal is beneficial as well. However, many development companies will only accept applicants with a bachelor's degree or higher. An advanced degree displays formal training and commitment to self-improvement. Higher education can also lead to contacts in the industry.

Game artistry is a competitive field. Standing out from the crowd can help get your work seen and appreciated. No two career paths will look the same, but everyone starts at the bottom and works their way up. As you prove yourself, you receive more opportunities and tasks and may be able to specialize more in your favorite areas. Leadership roles over a group of artists or even the whole department could even be in the cards. Game artistry is expanding quickly, expected to

Animators can work in a wide variety of fields, from TV and film to advertising and video game creation.

grow 4 percent between 2023 and 2033.

Many animation jobs are involved with making a game. Some work on special effects, while others animate dramatic cutscenes. Some *animators* specialize in worldbuilding, making sure everything in the game follows the same rules of nature and physics. And others work on ensuring the humans in the game look like real people when they walk and talk. Animators create libraries of those movements so that each character's mannerisms are consistent.

Games with first-person perspectives have different animation needs than third person. Details such as a character's arm length can sell a game or make it look cheesy. *First-person animators* must get the proper eye level and viewing ratio for the character correct. Both first- and *third-*

person animators are knowledgeable in animation software and game building. But first-person animators are usually more experienced in the field.

It's the *gameplay animator's* job to make sure impressive animations respond to every command players input. If there is a chance to add an interactive moment, the gameplay animator ensures the game animation and the cutscene animation flow smoothly. These animators work closely with every other department and have a high attention to detail. A strong background in cinematography and motion capture is necessary, as well as experience with combat system animations and choreography.

Visual effects (VFX) animators work with explosions, collisions, and every other special, physical moment that enhances the game. Even little details, such as a cloud of dust that bursts around a player when they land after a jump, a moth lingering around a torch, or a rippling stream, are VFX. VFX are also part of the UI and HUD effects, such as health bars and interactive elements including item pickups and spell casts. VFX artists are in high demand, with jobs available all over the world.

Two-year associate's degrees in video game design or computer animation are usually the minimum requirement for any animator, but a bachelor's degree will broaden your skillset and available jobs. There are also ways to learn about animation online. Courses from places such as Udemy and Skillshare can expand your knowledge of software and technologies. Animators make a wide range of salaries depending on experience, but the average is around $99,000.

A Virtual World with Real Jobs

Some people believe the future of gaming is virtual reality (VR) and augmented reality (AR). People have been playing *Pokémon Go* and enjoying photo and video filters for years. Many have tried virtual reality through Oculus and Meta Quest and strapped on PlayStation's VR2 headsets. And the market continues to grow. In 2024 there were fewer than a million jobs in the VR industry. But by 2030, there will be a projected twenty-three million. Around $12 billion was spent on VR and AR tech in 2020. Four years later, that number had jumped to more than $60 billion.

There are many possibilities for jumping into the VR development world. Software engineers and product designers are always needed. But there are also jobs in AI research, electrical engineering and manufacturing, and environmental health and safety.

Creating a game that both looks good and is fun to play is a challenge that game designers must tackle.

Game designers develop the game's plot, world rules, objectives, and characters. They build the game's mechanics and have an end goal of a seamless user experience. Game designers need both artistic and technical skills. They work closely with the rest of the creative team to ensure every piece flows together.

Systems designers make sure the nitty-gritty parts of the game stay realistic and consistent. Is the amount of gold you collect enough to make necessary improvements to your character? Is the amount of damage you take on a mission too high, or does it make the quest too easy? Does a heavy battle axe swing the same way as a light sword? The job details are ever-changing, but the role is the same—ensuring consistency.

Content designers put detail and creativity into the game. They flesh out quests and figure out what players need to do to finish them, make sure the NPCs are the correct ones for the story, write player tips and item descriptions, and detail other design features. Familiarity with scripting languages such as Lua is a plus.

Technical designers must understand the entire game and identify and fix any problems encountered. They come up with a process to fix gameplay problems and implement changes. A strong grasp of coding and computer science is important, as well as teamwork skills. Technical designers often bridge coders and design departments, so being able to explain why something doesn't work or explain a creative reason for a game feature is a must.

Sound designers are behind every noise you hear, from background music to the sound of armor as you run to the clink of coins being collected. They use sounds from commercial audio libraries or record their own. They record and edit dialogue and test sounds to make sure they work within the context of the game. A degree in audio engineering, as well as knowledge in sound software, game engines, coding, and composing are important. A strong portfolio will help get you noticed.

A bachelor's degree in graphic design, software engineering, computer science, or a similar field is usually necessary to become any kind of game designer, with a master's degree bringing potential for a higher payday. Game building, coding, and animation are all core skills. This field has a wide range of salaries, with location and experience being two major factors in pay. Average salaries begin around $57,000 but rise significantly with experience and time.

Ready to get started as a creative? As you've read, not all these jobs require a college degree, but an education helps develop and hone technical proficiency. One downside of creative jobs in the gaming industry is security. Jobs are tied to projects, and when the project ends, the job may too. Creative work can sometimes be unpredictable and unstable. A 2017 survey by the International Game Developers Association showed that professionals in the gaming industry had worked for an average of 2.2 employers over the past five years. Diversifying your skills and learning as much as you can while remaining flexible and prepared for change is key to helping find and sustain work.

CHAPTER FOUR
The Party

Creating a video game is a team effort. Everyone has different skills and abilities, and when they work together, something amazing gets made. Some gaming jobs focus on keeping things running smoothly.

The Leader

Project managers must be highly organized; have good leadership, negotiation, and problem-solving skills; be familiar with setting and sticking to budgets; and be comfortable with taking responsibility. A bachelor's degree is usually the minimum requirement for this role. It doesn't necessarily need to be in a gaming or computer industry—project management is similar across many industries. A master of business administration (MBA) or master's degree in video game production will give you an edge over the competition. The average salary for a project manager starts around $99,000. As more companies embrace VR, AI, and other new branches of the gaming world, the need for project managers continues to grow. Across all industries, a predicted twenty-five million project professionals will be needed by 2030.

The Helper

Even after a game is made, there is a lot of work to do. Some games, such as *Fortnite*, are always updating. Sometimes servers crash, or players lose their accounts. And no matter how much quality assurance and testing are done, glitches can sneak through. Who steps in after the game is released?

People in *information technology (IT)* provide technical support to both employees and players. They troubleshoot issues and make sure the game network stays safe from viruses and hackers. They ensure the game servers and

As more technology becomes part of our everyday lives, experts in IT will be even more important.

Ensuring players have a good experience in and out of the game creates more loyal customers.

operating systems are running efficiently. Problem-solving, communication, and a strong background in technology are important skills. While this job doesn't help with actually making the game, it does support the game's future. IT specialists make around $71,500 a year.

With more than three billion people around the world playing games, it is inevitable that someone would need help. *Customer service representatives (CSRs)* record any issues players report and pass them along to IT or game developers. CSRs also address comments left online, moderate forums and in-game chats, and answer any questions about the game. They must know the brand in and out and be available right away. The average salary for a senior CSR is $32,700.

There are many other jobs that can get you closer to a job in game creation and service. It is a huge industry. Voice-over acting, audio work, finance, coaching, scouting, team management, retail positions, and human resources are only a handful of the additional options available. Finding the right one is the first step toward your future.

CHAPTER FIVE

The Waiting Room: Professional Gamers

Playing games for fun is something a lot of people do. But others take it to the next level and get paid for doing what they love. Streamers, game testers, and pro gamers can earn income in various ways, from winning prizes to attracting audiences and gaining advertisement dollars to getting sponsorships from big companies to testing out new games for developers.

Twitch has more than 140 million active users who tune in to see their favorite players or their favorite games. In 2024, 2.4 million viewers logged on at any one time to watch ninety-nine thousand different channels streaming in that same moment. There were more than seven million active *streamers* to choose from. Some streamers only have subscribers, while others also have sponsors who pay the streamer to wear their merchandise or use their products. Giveaways are another way streamers can spread the word about their sponsors. Top streamers build a strong brand and have big personalities that engage their viewers.

At the lowest level, streamers might earn just $50 a

Being a professional gamer may sound like a new idea. But it has been a career since 1997!

month. But they can make much more. A YouTube content creator can make $15 for every one thousand ad views. Twitch streamers have followers who support them through subscriptions. Followers can also buy digital currency called Bits that they can redeem for emotes called Cheers. Streamers earn one cent for each Bit used in their chat. TikTok offers a similar streaming reaction monetization system, giving TikTokers a percent of the cut for each Live Gift their followers send.

Professional gamers compete in esports tournaments. They train just like a traditional athlete, drilling moves and specializing in one type of game. Some enjoy fighting games, while others like first-person shooters or racing games. There are games that allow players to join up as pairs or teams,

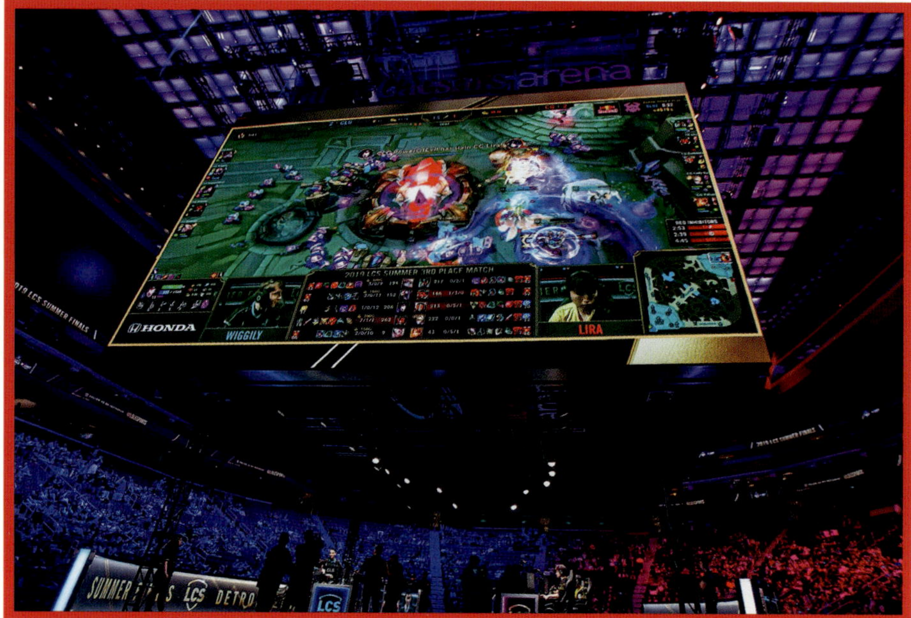

Thousands of people turn out to see their favorite competitive gamers face off in arena-style battles.

while others are completely on their own. Only around two thousand competitive gamers make a living doing what they love. The average salary is $60,000 a year. Many supplement this with sponsorships, ads, merch, and brand deals. Staying at the top of the gaming field is challenging and requires a huge time commitment. If you can't maintain your place at the top, your source of income quickly dries up. The average retirement age from the field is twenty-five since players often eventually choose to game part-time while getting a regular full-time job to pay the bills.

For the elite, though, the chance for a huge payout is appealing, especially as esports becomes more accepted as a form of competition. Professional gamers can earn anywhere from $250,000 to $1,000,000. But that number isn't always reflective of the industry as a whole.

"Money in esports is a tricky subject," said Andy "Andersin" Collins, an esports athlete who was once part of a pro team. He won a scholarship that paid for his undergraduate and master's degrees. But even at the highest level, he wasn't becoming a millionaire. "Many teams and players are either unpaid or paid less than minimum wage.... And sure, while some of *Valorant's* highest-earning players make 6-to-7 figures each year... that's simply not the norm." At his peak, Collins only made around $48,000 a year.

Want to become a pro gamer? You can start by joining tournaments and competitions. All online competitive games have global rankings or leaderboards that change every day.

Some *testers* work in quality assurance for big video game companies. Third-party testing companies hire others. Sometimes, testers play through the same part of a game repeatedly, trying to trigger certain glitches or scenarios. Other times, they just run around trying new things and looking for bugs. It can be a grind with a lot of repetition. There are also many low-paying positions, with the average salary at $26,000. But working as a tester can also be a way to work on video games from home without any experience, even if you are still in high school. And if you're dedicated, you may catch the eye of a big developer who can pay more.

From streaming to competing to testing, being a professional gamer does not require education or job experience. Hard work and talent are the main tools needed to thrive as a pro. Find a type of game you like, stick with it, and practice, practice, practice.

CHAPTER SIX

Open Your Map

If you have decided that a job in the video game industry is for you, it's time to start honing your skills. You probably already noticed common skills or backgrounds needed. Here are some expert tips and strategies that can set you up for a future playing, creating, fixing, and enjoying video games.

Choose Your Team

What is your favorite part of video games? If you like playing and are thinking of going pro, take it seriously. Set a schedule as you would for any other sport. Write out goals with concrete objectives such as "improve accuracy to ten hits a minute" or "beat level thirty seconds faster than before." If you like worldbuilding, write stories and make them as detailed as you can. Describe or draw what you think the characters should look like. Think up missions for them and the places they will go. If creation is more to your interests, give it a try. Game engines including Unity, Unreal, and

Learning how to build your own computer can be easy. Taking it to the next step by learning how to repair and solder hardware can give you even more of an edge for the future.

Godot are free to individuals. Watch tutorials or read books on coding. Join or start a gaming club at your school. And, most importantly, play a wide variety of different games! Nothing can tell you more about what works or doesn't in a game than playing one yourself.

Learning how to talk to other people and work well on a team are skills that will serve you well online and in the real world.

Mic On

Everyone needs communication skills, and being part of a game creation team is no different. Practice being a good listener and paying attention to both verbal and non-verbal cues. Pay attention in your language and literature glasses—they help teach you how to communicate effectively out loud and on paper. Ask for feedback at work or in school. Show others your creative works and ask for feedback, approaching constructive criticism with an open mind. Follow directions, but also don't be afraid to offer ideas on how processes could be improved. Take the kind of notes you would want to borrow. Listen to everyone on your team and remember that everyone has different layers of knowledge and expertise.

Be a Leader

Even if you do not have a management position, good project management can improve your work experience and productivity. Being organized and self-directed will serve you well in school and on the job. If you find your assertiveness or leadership lacking, work on honing your skills. Join the speech team or drama club or take a greater role in an activity or sport's team in which you are already involved. If you are shy, it might help to step up in a setting where nobody knows you. Volunteer to call BINGO at an assisted living facility or make cold calls for a nonprofit. Or volunteer or work at organizations with strong leadership and learn from people already doing the job.

Making friends with the same interests may sound like fun. But it can also open doors to new opportunities.

Join a Guild

There are many professional organizations out there, and each is full of industry professionals ready to mentor the next generation. The Entertainment Software Association, the Graphic Artists Guild, the Game Developers Guild, the Web Design Agency, and others protect and promote the interests of like-minded people interested in games, design, and graphic art. Visit their websites and watch for training opportunities, meet and greets, networking events, and trade shows that you can use as a springboard to connect with others.

War Games

Video games are not just for casual play. Some games are used for learning purposes too. The use of in-game design elements and principles outside their original use is called gamification. The United States armed forces have used virtual environments to train people on various maneuvers, formations, and drills. One game, *Full Spectrum Warrior*, was developed between game studio THQ Nordic and the army. Regular people could buy the game too, but a special code let enlisted military members access the in-game training information.

The armed forces also use gaming as a recruitment tool. They put out recruitment posters modeled after popular video game art. Recruiters can be found playing racing games such as *Rocket League* and first-person shooters. They have hosted *Fortnite* championships and made commercials featuring Meta Quest VR headsets. The navy spends 3 to 5 percent of their market budget—that's $4.3 million—on esports alone. And the army, air force, and coast guard have their own esports leagues. The marine corps have partnered with influencers in the gaming world to build their brand across social media.

Military esports teams allow students to interact with members of the armed forces and learn more about potential future opportunities through friendly competition.

Customize Your Skin

One way to get the attention of people in the gaming industry is on social media! Fan artists, cosplayers, streamers, and creators can build huge followings by just being themselves and sharing what they love with the world. Building up the confidence to go all in with your favorite things will give you a thick skin once you enter the professional creative world. It is also good practice for following another person's vision, bringing a fictional person or character to life, or expanding on a pre-existing world to be even more expansive than the original.

Level Up

There is always more to learn, and that is doubly true in an industry in which technology is rapidly advancing. Join a gaming club to improve your coding skills. Look for in-person learning opportunities through your school, community centers, or colleges. There are also low-cost or even free programs online that can teach you the basics. Outschool offers pre-recorded lessons or live online video classes divided by age. Tech companies and universities offer computer science certifications that people of any age can earn. Organizations including Kodeco, Codesmith, TripleTen, and the Linux Foundation even offer scholarships for their programs.

Get Smart

Once you know what part of the gaming industry you are interested in, you can focus on your academic future. For any

Learning from industry professionals can give you valuable information on what to expect in the future.

job that requires a college degree, first you'll have to obtain your high school degree or an equivalent general education diploma, commonly called a GED. As you're finishing high school, you can start applying to colleges. Many offer degrees in computer-related subjects. But which degree should you choose? Let's look at each field and how much it's growing to help you decide.

Audio engineering degrees prepare students for careers in recording studios, live recording, maintenance and operations, and other sound-collecting fields. This degree is a mixture of sound-related courses, practical math and engineering, and music history and performance classes.

Computer animation is usually a two-year degree, although some colleges offer it as part of their four-year programs. Courses familiarize students with Adobe and

Animation is all about your abilities. The more technique and technical understanding you have, the better your animation will be.

Open-Source software and both 2D and 3D animation. By the end of the program, students will have portfolios and demos to show off their skills. This degree can lead to jobs in the gaming or animation industries or can be used in a variety of other fields, such as advertising or marketing. Jobs for special effects artists and animators are predicted to grow 4 percent between 2023 and 2033.

Computer science is a common major that most colleges offer. Students learn how to build websites, write code, learn about operating systems, and more. They may specialize in robotics, network security, AI, software engineering, or something else. Internships, research opportunities, and more advanced degrees are all available on this path. Employment for computer science majors is projected to grow 13 percent from 2022 to 2026, adding 557,100 new jobs.

Computer engineering is a math-heavy program in which students learn about both hardware and software, including systems applications and electronic circuits. Programming languages, AI, robotics, and telecommunications are just a few areas of possible specialization. Employment for graduates is expected to grow by 7 percent from 2023 to 2033, and there is always demand for engineers as technology continues to advance.

Creative writing helps students perfect their reading, writing, and comprehension skills. They get an in-depth look at different genres of writing and give and receive feedback on their own work. Screenwriting is often a specialization within this major, although some colleges offer it as its own major. The Bureau of Labor Statistics projects that writers and authors will see job growth of 4 percent between 2022 and 2032.

Game development emphasizes programming languages and game design. Students learn development standards and tips to streamline production and testing. They also study trends in the industry, as well as creative subjects such as screenwriting basics and audio production. A 21 percent growth increase by 2028 means this field continues to grow and expand.

Graphic designers study a wide array of art, from history to different styles. They learn how to create graphics and illustrations and prepare layout files for advertisements, promotions, branding labels, and more. Many colleges offer graphic design programs. This field is steady, with a 2 percent growth outlook between 2023 and 2033.

Software engineers learn about coding and programming, but they also study math, chemistry, and physics, which are

Engineers must know the ins and outs of the computers they work with.

necessary when it comes to creating and maintaining software systems. Helping computers perform faster and smarter is their main goal. Students also get the chance to learn more about VR and game design. The Bureau of Labor Statistics says that overall employment of software developers, quality assurance analysts, and testers will grow 17 percent between 2023 and 2033.

Video game design is usually a two-year associate's degree. Students learn 2D and 3D animation concepts, use software they will need to know to work in the industry, and work on their own games. An estimated 32,090 new jobs in this field will need to be filled by 2029.

MBA degrees are the most advanced business graduate degrees. To earn a graduate degree, you must first earn an undergraduate degree, such as one of the ones listed above or a bachelor's degree in business. You can get a general MBA, but there are also more specialized MBAs, such as those in leadership, finance, business management, or marketing. A few MBA programs even specialize in game design. In 2022 MBA graduates saw an $85,000 increase in their salaries after earning their degree.

You can also get a master's degree in video game production. Other similar master's degrees go by names such as interactive media, games computing, game art, or game design and development. These advanced degrees explore the creation, improvement, and innovation behind games and build on previous development skills. Depending on the area of game design, career growth for manager-level developers is projected to grow 8 percent from 2023 to 2033.

Learn a New Language

There are hundreds—or even thousands—of coding languages that programmers have created. Some of the most popular for video games are C++, Java, C#, Python, and JavaScript. Starting out with easier languages such as Python or JavaScript can give you confidence and help you build a strong portfolio. Then you can see what types of games you are interested in and decide if taking the next step to learning a more difficult language is worth it. For example, Unreal Engine uses C++, while Unity uses C#. Each development company usually picks one or two and sticks with them, so researching game developers and what they use can help you decide which languages to learn too.

Kat Law, an engineer who teaches coding, looks at learning coding languages like learning spoken ones. "I don't believe coding is hard, but it can be intimidating at first. Like learning a new speaking language, different coding languages have their own unique nuances and challenges." But she says each language has similar fundamentals and algorithms, and once you have figured those out, learning and writing in them becomes much easier.

And like a spoken language, learning a coding language takes time and practice. As you learn the ins and outs of your chosen language, things will get easier, and your confidence will grow. You can also share coding projects with other people to receive feedback. Or you could team up with a friend or club to learn together.

CONCLUSION
Roll Credits

Video games aren't going anywhere, and as the ways we game continue to expand, so will the job market. Free-to-play gaming, which allows people access to games without an up-front cost, and cloud gaming, where games can be streamed without requiring expensive hardware, have already revolutionized this industry. The metaverse, once a place only described in science fiction books, is more real every day, with games such as *Fortnite* hosting virtual concerts and *Minecraft* allowing people to create and share new worlds with each other. We already have one foot in the door, with people watching Twitch streamers on their computer, entering a VR world by strapping on a headset, and casting the VR picture onto their TV—all at the same time.

The video game industry is huge, and no matter what your skills or interests, there is a job out there for you. You may be involved in the design of the next greatest video game franchise, help score its music, or boost its sales off the chart. Options to build the right path for you are as vast as an open world game. It might look like a lot to take in, but take your time, explore, and choose your own adventure.

GLOSSARY

campaign: an organized course of action to achieve a goal

certificate: an official document certifying that someone has fulfilled set requirements

computer-generated imagery: special effects created with computer software; also known as CGI

coding: the process or activity of writing computer programs

component: a part or element of a larger whole

computer chip: a tiny electronic device made up of multiple interconnected electrical components; also known as microchips or integrated circuits

console: an electronic machine used to play games

cutscene: a scene shown to the player when they reach a particular point in the game, such as before a battle or when the player's character dies

engine: software framework designed for the development of video games. Game engines have a library of code that makes it easier for users to create games because they don't have to start over from scratch.

esports: a multiplayer video game played competitively in front of spectators

framework: a basic building block of computer programming. Framework can be changed by additional user-written code for more specific uses.

franchise: a series of related video games

graphics: visual images made by computer processing

guild: an association of people working toward a common goal

hardware: the machines, wiring, and other physical components of a computer or gaming system

indie: a video game created by an individual or a small development team without financial or technical support from a large game publisher

intellectual property: a work or invention that is the result of creativity, such as an invention design, computer code, or artistic work

interface: a device or program that allows a user to connect with a computer

internship: a program in which a student or trainee works in an organization with or without pay to gain work experience

mechanics: the rules of a game that govern and guide the player's actions and the game's response to them

mentorship: a period of guidance or direction given by a more experienced person in an organization to a younger or less experienced person

metaverse: in computing, a persistent virtual environment that allows access to and interoperability of multiple individual virtual realities

model: a computer program that creates a model or simulation of something in the real world

network: a system that connects two or more computers for sending and sharing information

platform: the basic hardware and software on which applications can be run

portfolio: a collection of projects that best represent an artist's work

producer: a person who oversees production of a game

software: the programs and other operating systems used by a computer

streaming: broadcasting live gameplay over the internet, allowing viewers to watch and engage in real time

SOURCE NOTES

9 "No matter how . . . of the future": "The Future of Artificial Intelligence in Video Games," Columbia Engineering, September 2023, https://ai.engineering.columbia.edu/ai-applications/ai-video-games/#fn1b.

10 "handled it the . . . a positive outcome": "The Game Industry has Spoken: Remove vs. Hybrid vs. On-Site," *Deconstructor of Fun*, July 11, 2023, https://www.deconstructoroffun.com/blog/the-game-industry-has-spoken-remote-vs-hybrid-vs-on-site.

12 "The way we . . . in different studios.": Ben Wodecki Jr., "What Other Industries Can Learn from Video Game Innovation," AI Business, December 7, 2022, https://aibusiness.com/ml/what-other-industries-can-learn-from-video-game-innovation#close-modal.

20 "This is one . . . of using digital.": "Game Design: An Interview with Barthelemy Atsin and Nelle Stokes," Long Island High School for the Arts, March 2021, https://www.longislandhighschoolforthearts.org/blog/game-design-interview-with-barthelemy-atsin-and-nelle-stokes/.

41 "Many teams and . . . not the norm.": Madison Hall, "I'm a 26-Year-Old Software Engineer Making $75,000, and Still Dream of Becoming a Professional E-Sports Athlete. Here's How I Balance Work and My Gaming Endeavors," *Business Insider*, April 27, 2024, https://www.businessinsider.com/i-work-8-to-5-job-to-supplement-esports-career-2024-4.

54 "I don't believe . . . nuances and challenges.": Team Multiverse, "Is Coding Hard to Learn? What Developers Say," *Multiverse*, June 1, 2023, https://www.multiverse.io/en-US/blog/is-coding-hard.

SELECTED BIBLIOGRAPHY

"The Complete List of Gaming Jobs." Hitmarker, July 4, 2022. https://hitmarker.net/career-advice/the-complete-list-of-gaming-jobs.

Padmore, William. "Growth in Esports Paves New Career Paths Beyond the Screen." Nebraska Public Media, March 23, 2023. https://nebraskapublicmedia.org/en/news/news-articles/growth-in-esports-paves-new-career-paths-beyond-the-screen/.

Perna, Mark C. "Why More Employers Want to Hire People Based on Their Video Game Skills." *Forbes*, November 14, 2023. https://www.forbes.com/sites/markcperna/2023/11/14/why-more-employers-want-to-hire-people-based-on-their-video-game-skills/.

Schwartzburg, Rosa. "The US Military Is Embedded in the Gaming World. Its Target: Teen Recruits." *Guardian*, February 14, 2024. https://www.theguardian.com/us-news/2024/feb/14/us-military-recruiting-video-games-targeting-teenagers.

Wakefield, Jane. "How the Computer Games Industry Is Embracing AI." BBC, May 2, 2024. https://www.bbc.com/news/business-68844761.

"Your Guide to the Different Career Pathways You Can Take in the Game Development Industry." *Circuit Stream*, March 30, 2022. https://www.circuitstream.com/blog/your-guide-to-the-different-career-pathways-you-can-take-in-the-game-development-industry.

FURTHER INFORMATION

Books

Gregory, Josh. *Fortnite: Year Eight.* Ann Arbor, MI: Cherry Lake, 2025.
Take an in-depth look at the latest features in *Fortnite* and the game's success.

Morkes, Andrew. *Exploring Engineering Careers.* Minneapolis: Twenty-First Century Books, 2026.
Discover a variety of engineering career pathways and how to start preparing for a career in engineering during your high school years.

Olson, Elsie. *AI Basics.* Minneapolis: Lerner Publications, 2025.
Learn about the past, present, and future of AI.

Romphf, Joshua. *Coding Activities for Developing Games in Unity.* New York: Rosen, 2022.
Learn coding skills that will be useful in game development, as well as overall computer literacy.

Streissguth, Tom. *Making Video Games.* Minneapolis: ABDO, 2024.
Take a look at the difference between game developers, as well as the challenges and skills it takes to make a video game.

Vale, Jenna. *Get Coding with Minecraft.* Buffalo: Gareth Sevens, 2024.
Learn how to code using logic, coding, and STEM skills in the world of *Minecraft*.

Websites

ComputerScience.org

https://www.computerscience.org/careers/video-game-designer/
Explore paths to getting a job in the gaming industry, read about trends, and learn career-building strategies.

Game Industry Career Guide

https://www.gameindustrycareerguide.com/video-game-careers/
This site summarizes some of the careers related to game development, as well as related jobs within each field.

Indie Game Developer Network

https://www.igdnonline.com/
The Indie Game Developer Network is an international volunteer trade organization that supports indie game developers in all gaming formats.

International Game Developers Association

https://igda.org/
The International Game Developers Association is the world's largest nonprofit organization serving people who create games.

Network of Academic and Scholastic Esports Federations

https://www.nasef.org/career-pathways
Explore some of the career pathways related to scholastic esports that include—but are not exclusive to—players and the games themselves.

INDEX

ABOUT THE AUTHORS

Sherry Howard is a freelance author from Middletown, Kentucky. She enjoys writing poetry, fiction, and nonfiction for children. When she's not writing, you might find her chatting with grandchildren, playing with pampered pups, enjoying the fish's colors in her aquariums, or feeding a bearded dragon named Kuda. She's a big fan of southern front porches, the roar of ocean waves, and the wisdom of Yoda.

Mari Bolte has loved video games since she brought her first GameCube home. She writes and edits books for kids in every possible subject, which unfortunately takes up all her game time. Thank goodness for streaming.

PHOTO ACKNOWLEDGMENTS

Image credits: Alistair Berg/Digital Vision/Getty Images, p.5; visualspace/E+/Getty Images, p.7; Gorodenkoff/Shutterstock, p.15; Ростислав Початенко/Getty Images, p.16; gorodenkoff/iStock/Getty Images, p. 21; Dutchmen Photography/Shutterstock, p.23; lechatnoir/E+/Getty Images, p.24; Chaosamran_Stuido/iStock/Getty Images, p.27; Pixel-Shot/Shutterstock, p.29; NoSystem Images/E+/Getty Images, p.31; zeljkosantrac/E+/Getty Images, p.32; Luis Alvarez/DigitalVision/Getty Images, p.36; Tetra Images/Getty Images, p.37; PASCAL GUYOT/AFP/Getty Images, p.39; Dave Reginek/Getty Images Sport/Getty Images, p.40; vm/E+/Getty Images, p.43; mixetto/E+/Getty Images, p.44; Diamond Dogs/iStock/Getty Images, p.46; Karen Warren/Houston Chronicle/Hearst/Getty Images, p.47; Laurence Dutton/E+/Getty Images, p.49; Addictive Stock/iStock/Getty Images, p.50; Authentic Images/E+/Getty Images, p.52.

Cover image: hobo_018/E+/Getty Images